THE TALKING DONKEY IN THE BOOK OF NUMBERS - REVISED

WHAT DOES THIS ALLEGORICAL STORY SAY TO US TODAY?

Michael Harvey Koplitz

Hebraic Analysis

Introduction

A problem with many people when it comes to the Bible is the interpretation of the stories that it contains. In today's technological world, believing that a donkey spoke to its human rider is difficult. The story of thirteen-year-old David defeating a nine-foot guy named Goliath is also difficult to believe. The problem today is that our western Greek-influenced world is reading a document written thousands of years ago using Semitic methods. The church has been interpreting the Bible using its Greek-western philosophies and understandings and offering bizarre explanations to the stories at times.

Semitic people wrote stories in the Bible in allegorical form. Therefore, reading the stories in a purely literal form does not give the original author's intent. Besides, the culture of ancient Israel, Babylon, and Persia are in the stories but are not spelled out. To fully understand a biblical story, the cultural background of the author's time must be considered.

One of the newer biblical interpretation methods being taught in seminary is to read a book of the Bible literally. This way of reading does not consider the allegorical method of the author's writing, the language's idioms, and indeed not the culture of the time. This method leaves for an interpretation of the story that does not coincide with the author's original intention.

The Greek-western interpretation of the Bible does not offer the word's original meaning. How should the Bible be interpreted? Ancient Bible Study Methods must be used to understand biblical stories.

Numbers chapter twenty-two is the beginning of the story of Balak and Balaam. This book deals directly with the story of the talking donkey; therefore, the presentation is the interpretation of chapter twenty-two using Ancient Bible Study Methods. Several articles are included in the book to help the reader understand the difference between Greek (western) and Hebraic learning methods. A further reference book for a deeper understanding of this method is "What Are Ancient Bible Study Methods? An exploration of the Bible study methods used in the time of Yeshua" by the author and available through Amazon.

The main differences between the Greek method and the Hebraic method of teaching

Once a student becomes aware of these two teaching styles, the student will be able to determine if the class attended or if a book read is in either Greek or Hebraic. In the Greek manner, the instructor is always right because of advanced knowledge. In the college situation, it is because the professor has his/her Ph.D. in some area of study, so one assumes that he or she knows everything about the topic. For example, Rodney Dangerfield played the role of a middle-aged man going to college. His English midterm was to write about Kurt Vonnegut Jr. Since he did not understand any of Vonnegut's books, he hired Vonnegut himself to write the midterm. When he received the paper from the English Professor told Dangerfield that whoever wrote the paper knew nothing about Vonnegut. The professor's words are an example of the Greek method of teaching. Did the Ph.D. English professor think that she knew more about Vonnegut's writings than Vonnegut did. [1]

In the Greek teaching method, the professor or the instructor claims to be the authority. If one attends a Bible study class and the class leader says, "I will teach you the only way to understand this biblical book," you may want to consider the implications. This method is standard since most Seminaries and Bible colleges teach a Greek mode of learning, which

---

[1] *Back to School.* Performed by Rodney Dangerfield. Hollywood: CA: Paper Clip Productions, 1986. DVD.

is the same method the church has been utilizing for centuries.

Hebraic teaching methods are different. The teacher wants the students to challenge what they hear. It is through questioning that a student can learn. Also, the teacher wants his/her students to excel to the point where the student becomes the teacher.

If two rabbis come together to discuss a passage of Scripture, the result will be at least ten different opinions. All points of view are acceptable if each is supported by biblical evidence. It is permissible and encouraged that students develop many ideas. There is a depth to God's Word, and God wants us to find all His messages contained in the Scripture.

Seeking out the meaning of the Scriptures beyond the literal meaning is essential to understand God's Word fully.[2] The Greek method of learning the Scriptures has prevailed over the centuries. One problem is that only the literal interpretation of Scripture was often viewed as valid, as prompted by Martin Luther's "sola literalis," meaning that just the literal translation of Scripture was accurate. The Fundamentalist movements of today base their beliefs on the literal interpretation of the Scripture. Therefore, they do not believe that God placed more profound, hidden, or secret meanings in the Word.

---

[2] Davis, Anne Kimball. *The Synoptic Gospels*. MP3. Albuquerque: NM: BibleInteract, 2012.

The students of the Scriptures who learn through Hebraic training and understanding have drawn a different conclusion. The Hebrew language itself leads to different possible interpretations because of the construction of the language. The Hebraic method of Bible study opens avenues of thought about God's revelations in the Scripture never considered. Not all questions about the Scripture studied will have an immediate answer. If so, it becomes the responsibility of the learners to uncover the meaning. Also, remember that many opinions about the meaning of Scripture are also acceptable.

Michael Harvey Koplitz

Methodology

The methodology employed is to use First Century Scripture study methods integrated with the customs and culture of Yeshua's day to examine the Hebrew and Christian Scriptures, thus gathering a more in-depth understanding by learning the Scriptures in the way the people of Yeshua's day did.

I have titled the methodology of analyzing a passage of Scripture in a Hebraic manner, the "Process of Discovery." The author developed this methodology, which brings together various areas of linguistic and cultural understanding. There are several sections to the process, and not all the parts apply to every passage of Scripture. The overall result of developing this process is to give the reader a framework for studying the word in more depth.

The "Process of Discovery" starts with a Scripture passage. An examination of the linguistic structure of the passage is next. The linguistic structure includes parallelism, chiastic structures, and repetition. Formatting the passage in its linguistic form allows the reader to be able to visualize what the first century CE listener was hearing. Their corresponding sections label the chiasms, for example, A, B, C, B', A.' Not all passages of the Scriptures have a poetic form.

The next step is to "question the narrative." The questioning of the narrative process assuming the reader knows nothing about the passage. Therefore, the questions go from the simple to the complex. The next task is to identify any linguistic patterns. Linguistic patterns include, but are not limited to irony, simile, metaphor, symbolism, idioms, hyperbole, figurative language, personification, and allegory.

A review of any translation inconsistencies discovered between the English NAU version and either the Hebrew or Greek versions is done. There are times when a Hebrew or Greek word is translated in more than one way. Inconsistencies also can be created by the translation committee, which may have decided to use traditional language instead of the actual translation. The decision of the translation committee is in the Preface or Introduction to the Bible. Perhaps some of the inconsistencies were intentionally added to convey some deeper meaning. An examination for every discrepancy is done.

The passage is analyzed for any echoes of the Hebrew Scriptures in the Christian Scriptures. Using a passage from the Hebrew Scriptures in the Christian Scriptures, an echo occurs.[3] Also, echoes are found when Torah (Genesis through Deuteronomy) passages are used in other Hebrew Bible books. Cross-references in the Scripture are references from one verse to

---

[3] Mitzvot are the 613 commandments found in the Torah that please God. There are positive and negative commandments. The list was first development by Maimonides. The full list can be found at: ttp://www.jewfaq.org/613.htm.

another verse, which can assist the reader in understanding the verse.

The names of persons mentioned in the passage are listed. Many of the Hebrew names have meaning and may be associated with places or actions. Jewish parents used to name their children based on what they felt God had in store for their child. An example of this is Abraham, whose original name was Abram and was changed to mean eternal father (God changed Abram's name to Abraham, indicating a function he was to perform). When the Hebrew Bible gives names, many of the occurrences mean something unique. The same importance can occur for the names of places. The time it takes to travel between locations can supply insight into the event.

Keyphrases are identified in verses when they are essential to an understanding of that passage. There are no rules for selecting the keywords. Searching for other occurrences of the keywords in Scripture in a concordance is necessary to understand the word's usage; this must be done in either Hebrew or Greek, not in English. A classic Hebraic approach is to find the usage of a word in the Scripture by finding other verses that contain the word. The usage of a word, in its original language, is discovered by searching the Scripture in the language of the word. Verses that contain the word are identified, and a pattern for the usage of the word discovered. Each verse is examined to see what the usage of the word is which, may reveal a model for the word's usage. For Hebrew words, the first usage of the word in the Scripture, primarily if used in the

Torah, is essential. For the Greek words, the Christian Scriptures are used to determine the word usage in the Scripture. Sometimes finding the equivalent Greek word in the Septuagint then analyzing its usage in Hebrew can be very helpful.

The Rules of Hillel are used when applicable. Hillel was a Torah scholar who lived shortly before Yeshua's day. Hillel developed several rules for Torah students to interpret the Scriptures, which refer to halachic Midrash. In several cases, these rules are helpful in the analysis of the Scripture.

The cultural implications from the period of the writing are done after the linguistic analysis is completed. The culture is crucial because it is not explicitly referenced in the biblical narratives, as indicated earlier.

From the linguistic analysis and the cultural understanding, it is possible to obtain a deeper meaning of the Scripture beyond the literal meaning of the plain text. That is what the listeners of Yeshua's time were doing. They put the linguistics and culture together without even having to contemplate it.

The analysis will lead to a set of findings explaining what the passage meant in Yeshua's day. Most of the time, the Hebraic analysis leads to the desire for more in-depth analysis to fully understand what Yeshua was talking about or what was happening to Him. Whatever the result, a new, more in-depth understanding of the Scripture is obtained.

The components of the Process of Discovery are:

Language

Process of Discovery

Linguistics Section

Linguistic Structure

Discussion

Questioning the Passage

Verse Comparison of citations or proof text

Translation Inconsistencies

Biblical Personalities

Biblical Locations

Phrase Study

Only the application sections are included in this document.

Language – Numbers Chapter 22

New American Standard 1995	Hebrew
1 Then the sons of Israel journeyed, and camped in the plains of Moab beyond the Jordan *opposite* Jericho. 2 Now Balak the son of Zippor saw all that Israel had done to the Amorites. 3 So Moab was in great fear because of the people, for they were numerous; and Moab was in dread of the sons of Israel. 4 Moab said to the elders of Midian, "Now this horde will lick up all that is around us, as the ox licks up the grass of	וַיִּסְעוּ בְּנֵי יִשְׂרָאֵל וַיַּחֲנוּ בְּעַרְבוֹת מוֹאָב מֵעֵבֶר לְיַרְדֵּן יְרֵחוֹ׃ ס 2וַיַּרְא בָּלָק בֶּן־צִפּוֹר אֵת כָּל־אֲשֶׁר־עָשָׂה יִשְׂרָאֵל לָאֱמֹרִי׃ 3וַיָּגָר מוֹאָב מִפְּנֵי הָעָם מְאֹד כִּי רַב־הוּא וַיָּקָץ מוֹאָב מִפְּנֵי בְּנֵי יִשְׂרָאֵל׃ 4וַיֹּאמֶר מוֹאָב אֶל־זִקְנֵי מִדְיָן עַתָּה יְלַחֲכוּ הַקָּהָל אֶת־כָּל־סְבִיבֹתֵינוּ כִּלְחֹךְ הַשּׁוֹר אֵת יֶרֶק הַשָּׂדֶה וּבָלָק בֶּן־צִפּוֹר מֶלֶךְ לְמוֹאָב בָּעֵת הַהִוא׃ 5וַיִּשְׁלַח מַלְאָכִים אֶל־בִּלְעָם בֶּן־בְּעוֹר פְּתוֹרָה אֲשֶׁר עַל־הַנָּהָר אֶרֶץ בְּנֵי־עַמּוֹ

the field." And Balak the son of Zippor was king of Moab at that time.

5 So he sent messengers to Balaam the son of Beor, at Pethor, which is near the River, *in* the land of the sons of his people, to call him, saying, "Behold, a people came out of Egypt; behold, they cover the surface of the land, and they are living opposite me.

6 "Now, therefore, please come, curse this people for me since they are too mighty for me; perhaps I may be able to defeat them and drive them out of the land. For I know that he whom you bless is blessed, and he

לִקְרֹא־לֹו לֵאמֹר הִנֵּה עַם יָצָא מִמִּצְרַיִם הִנֵּה כִסָּה אֶת־עֵין הָאָרֶץ וְהוּא יֹשֵׁב מִמֻּלִי:

6 וְעַתָּה לְכָה־נָּא אָרָה־לִּי אֶת־הָעָם הַזֶּה כִּי־עָצוּם הוּא מִמֶּנִּי אוּלַי אוּכַל נַכֶּה־בֹּו וַאֲגָרְשֶׁנּוּ מִן־הָאָרֶץ כִּי יָדַעְתִּי אֵת אֲשֶׁר־תְּבָרֵךְ מְבֹרָךְ וַאֲשֶׁר תָּאֹר יוּאָר:

7 וַיֵּלְכוּ זִקְנֵי מוֹאָב וְזִקְנֵי מִדְיָן וּקְסָמִים בְּיָדָם וַיָּבֹאוּ אֶל־בִּלְעָם וַיְדַבְּרוּ אֵלָיו דִּבְרֵי בָלָק:

8 וַיֹּאמֶר אֲלֵיהֶם לִינוּ פֹה הַלַּיְלָה וַהֲשִׁבֹתִי אֶתְכֶם דָּבָר כַּאֲשֶׁר יְדַבֵּר יְהוָה אֵלָי וַיֵּשְׁבוּ שָׂרֵי־מוֹאָב עִם־בִּלְעָם:

9 וַיָּבֹא אֱלֹהִים אֶל־בִּלְעָם וַיֹּאמֶר מִי

whom you curse is cursed." 7 So the elders of Moab and the elders of Midian departed with the *fees for* divination in their hand; and they came to Balaam and repeated Balak's words to him. 8 He said to them, "Spend the night here, and I will bring word back to you as the LORD may speak to me." And the leaders of Moab stayed with Balaam. 9 Then God came to Balaam and said, "Who are these men with you?" 10 Balaam said to God, "Balak the son of Zippor, king of Moab, has sent *word* to me, 11 'Behold, there is a people who came out	הָאֲנָשִׁים הָאֵלֶּה עִמָּךְ׃ 10 וַיֹּאמֶר בִּלְעָם אֶל־הָאֱלֹהִים בָּלָק בֶּן־צִפֹּר מֶלֶךְ מוֹאָב שָׁלַח אֵלָי׃ 11 הִנֵּה הָעָם הַיֹּצֵא מִמִּצְרַיִם וַיְכַס אֶת־עֵין הָאָרֶץ עַתָּה לְכָה קָבָה־לִּי אֹתוֹ אוּלַי אוּכַל לְהִלָּחֶם בּוֹ וְגֵרַשְׁתִּיו׃ 12 וַיֹּאמֶר אֱלֹהִים אֶל־בִּלְעָם לֹא תֵלֵךְ עִמָּהֶם לֹא תָאֹר אֶת־הָעָם כִּי בָרוּךְ הוּא׃ 13 וַיָּקָם בִּלְעָם בַּבֹּקֶר וַיֹּאמֶר אֶל־שָׂרֵי בָלָק לְכוּ אֶל־אַרְצְכֶם כִּי מֵאֵן יְהֹוָה לְתִתִּי לַהֲלֹךְ עִמָּכֶם׃ 14 וַיָּקוּמוּ שָׂרֵי מוֹאָב וַיָּבֹאוּ אֶל־בָּלָק וַיֹּאמְרוּ מֵאֵן בִּלְעָם הֲלֹךְ עִמָּנוּ׃

of Egypt and they cover the surface of the land; now come, curse them for me; perhaps I may be able to fight against them and drive them out.'"

[12] God said to Balaam, "Do not go with them; you shall not curse the people, for they are blessed."

[13] So Balaam arose in the morning and said to Balak's leaders, "Go back to your land, for the LORD has refused to let me go with you."

[14] The leaders of Moab arose and went to Balak and said, "Balaam refused to come with us."

[15] Then Balak again sent leaders, more numerous and more distinguished than the former.

וַיֹּסֶף עוֹד בָּלָק [15] שְׁלֹחַ שָׂרִים רַבִּים וְנִכְבָּדִים מֵאֵלֶּה: וַיָּבֹאוּ אֶל־בִּלְעָם [16] וַיֹּאמְרוּ לוֹ כֹּה אָמַר בָּלָק בֶּן־צִפּוֹר אַל־נָא תִמָּנַע מֵהֲלֹךְ אֵלָי: כִּי־כַבֵּד אֲכַבֶּדְךָ [17] מְאֹד וְכֹל אֲשֶׁר־ תֹּאמַר אֵלַי אֶעֱשֶׂה וּלְכָה־נָּא קָבָה־לִּי אֵת הָעָם הַזֶּה: וַיַּעַן בִּלְעָם וַיֹּאמֶר [18] אֶל־עַבְדֵי בָלָק אִם־ יִתֶּן־לִי בָלָק מְלֹא בֵיתוֹ כֶּסֶף וְזָהָב לֹא אוּכַל לַעֲבֹר אֶת־פִּי יְהוָה אֱלֹהָי לַעֲשׂוֹת קְטַנָּה אוֹ גְדוֹלָה: וְעַתָּה שְׁבוּ נָא [19] בָזֶה גַּם־אַתֶּם הַלָּיְלָה וְאֵדְעָה מַה־יֹּסֵף יְהוָה דַּבֵּר עִמִּי: וַיָּבֹא אֱלֹהִים אֶל־ [20] בִּלְעָם לַיְלָה וַיֹּאמֶר לוֹ אִם־לִקְרֹא לְךָ בָּאוּ הָאֲנָשִׁים קוּם לֵךְ

¹⁶ They came to Balaam and said to him, "Thus says Balak the son of Zippor, 'Let nothing, I beg you, hinder you from coming to me;

¹⁷ for I will indeed honor you richly, and I will do whatever you say to me. Please come then, curse this people for me.'"

¹⁸ Balaam replied to the servants of Balak, "Though Balak were to give me his house full of silver and gold, I could not do anything, either small or great, contrary to the command of the LORD my God.

¹⁹ "Now please, you also stay here tonight, and I will find out what else the LORD will speak to me."

אַתֶּם וְאַךְ אֶת־הַדָּבָר אֲשֶׁר־אֲדַבֵּר אֵלֶיךָ אֹתוֹ תַעֲשֶׂה: ²¹ וַיָּקָם בִּלְעָם בַּבֹּקֶר וַיַּחֲבֹשׁ אֶת־אֲתֹנוֹ וַיֵּלֶךְ עִם־שָׂרֵי מוֹאָב: ²² וַיִּחַר־אַף אֱלֹהִים כִּי־הוֹלֵךְ הוּא וַיִּתְיַצֵּב מַלְאַךְ יְהוָה בַּדֶּרֶךְ לְשָׂטָן לוֹ וְהוּא רֹכֵב עַל־אֲתֹנוֹ וּשְׁנֵי נְעָרָיו עִמּוֹ: ²³ וַתֵּרֶא הָאָתוֹן אֶת־מַלְאַךְ יְהוָה נִצָּב בַּדֶּרֶךְ וְחַרְבּוֹ שְׁלוּפָה בְּיָדוֹ וַתֵּט הָאָתוֹן מִן־הַדֶּרֶךְ וַתֵּלֶךְ בַּשָּׂדֶה וַיַּךְ בִּלְעָם אֶת־הָאָתוֹן לְהַטֹּתָהּ הַדָּרֶךְ: ²⁴ וַיַּעֲמֹד מַלְאַךְ יְהוָה בְּמִשְׁעוֹל הַכְּרָמִים גָּדֵר מִזֶּה וְגָדֵר מִזֶּה: ²⁵ וַתֵּרֶא הָאָתוֹן אֶת־מַלְאַךְ יְהוָה וַתִּלָּחֵץ אֶל־הַקִּיר וַתִּלְחַץ

20 God came to Balaam at night and said to him, "If the men have come to call you, rise up *and* go with them; but only the word which I speak to you shall you do."

21 So Balaam arose in the morning, and saddled his donkey and went with the leaders of Moab.

22 But God was angry because he was going, and the angel of the LORD took his stand in the way as an adversary against him. Now he was riding on his donkey and his two servants were with him.

23 When the donkey saw the angel of the LORD standing in the way with his drawn

אֶת־רֶגֶל בִּלְעָם אֶל־הַקִּיר וַיֹּסֶף לְהַכֹּתָהּ:
26 וַיּוֹסֶף מַלְאַךְ־יְהוָה עֲבוֹר וַיַּעֲמֹד בְּמָקוֹם צָר אֲשֶׁר אֵין־דֶּרֶךְ לִנְטוֹת יָמִין וּשְׂמֹאול:
27 וַתֵּרֶא הָאָתוֹן אֶת־מַלְאַךְ יְהוָה וַתִּרְבַּץ תַּחַת בִּלְעָם וַיִּחַר־אַף בִּלְעָם וַיַּךְ אֶת־הָאָתוֹן בַּמַּקֵּל:
28 וַיִּפְתַּח יְהוָה אֶת־פִּי הָאָתוֹן וַתֹּאמֶר לְבִלְעָם מֶה־עָשִׂיתִי לְךָ כִּי הִכִּיתַנִי זֶה שָׁלֹשׁ רְגָלִים:
29 וַיֹּאמֶר בִּלְעָם לָאָתוֹן כִּי הִתְעַלַּלְתְּ בִּי לוּ יֶשׁ־חֶרֶב בְּיָדִי כִּי עַתָּה הֲרַגְתִּיךְ:
30 וַתֹּאמֶר הָאָתוֹן אֶל־בִּלְעָם הֲלוֹא אָנֹכִי אֲתֹנְךָ אֲשֶׁר־רָכַבְתָּ עָלַי מֵעוֹדְךָ עַד־הַיּוֹם הַזֶּה הַהַסְכֵּן הִסְכַּנְתִּי לַעֲשׂוֹת לְךָ כֹּה וַיֹּאמֶר לֹא:

sword in his hand, the donkey turned off from the way and went into the field; but Balaam struck the donkey to turn her back into the way.

24 Then the angel of the LORD stood in a narrow path of the vineyards, *with* a wall on this side and a wall on that side.

25 When the donkey saw the angel of the LORD, she pressed herself to the wall and pressed Balaam's foot against the wall, so he struck her again.

26 The angel of the LORD went further, and stood in a narrow place where there was no way to turn to the right hand or the left.

27 When the donkey saw the angel of the

31 וַיְגַ֣ל יְהֹוָה֮ אֶת־עֵינֵ֣י בִלְעָם֒ וַיַּ֞רְא אֶת־מַלְאַ֤ךְ יְהֹוָה֙ נִצָּ֣ב בַּדֶּ֔רֶךְ וְחַרְבּ֥וֹ שְׁלֻפָ֖ה בְּיָד֑וֹ וַיִּקֹּ֥ד וַיִּשְׁתַּ֖חוּ לְאַפָּֽיו:

32 וַיֹּ֣אמֶר אֵלָיו֮ מַלְאַ֣ךְ יְהֹוָה֒ עַל־מָ֗ה הִכִּ֙יתָ֙ אֶת־אֲתֹ֣נְךָ֔ זֶ֖ה שָׁל֣וֹשׁ רְגָלִ֑ים הִנֵּ֤ה אָֽנֹכִי֙ יָצָ֣אתִי לְשָׂטָ֔ן כִּֽי־יָרַ֥ט הַדֶּ֖רֶךְ לְנֶגְדִּֽי:

33 וַתִּרְאַ֙נִי֙ הָֽאָת֔וֹן וַתֵּ֣ט לְפָנַ֔י זֶ֖ה שָׁלֹ֣שׁ רְגָלִ֑ים אוּלַי֙ נָטְתָ֣ה מִפָּנַ֔י כִּ֥י עַתָּ֛ה גַּם־אֹתְכָ֥ה הָרַ֖גְתִּי וְאוֹתָ֥הּ הֶחֱיֵֽיתִי:

34 וַיֹּ֨אמֶר בִּלְעָ֜ם אֶל־מַלְאַ֤ךְ יְהֹוָה֙ חָטָ֔אתִי כִּ֣י לֹ֤א יָדַ֙עְתִּי֙ כִּ֥י אַתָּ֛ה נִצָּ֥ב לִקְרָאתִ֖י בַּדָּ֑רֶךְ וְעַתָּ֛ה אִם־רַ֥ע בְּעֵינֶ֖יךָ אָשׁ֥וּבָה לִּֽי:

35 וַיֹּ֩אמֶר֩ מַלְאַ֨ךְ יְהֹוָ֜ה אֶל־בִּלְעָ֗ם לֵ֚ךְ עִם־הָ֣אֲנָשִׁ֔ים וְאֶ֗פֶס אֶת־

LORD, she lay down under Balaam; so Balaam was angry and struck the donkey with his stick.

28 And the LORD opened the mouth of the donkey, and she said to Balaam, "What have I done to you, that you have struck me these three times?"

29 Then Balaam said to the donkey, "Because you have made a mockery of me! If there had been a sword in my hand, I would have killed you by now."

30 The donkey said to Balaam, "Am I not your donkey on which you have ridden all your life to this day? Have I ever been accustomed to do so

הַדָּבָר אֲשֶׁר־אֲדַבֵּר אֵלֶיךָ אֹתוֹ תְדַבֵּר וַיֵּלֶךְ בִּלְעָם עִם־שָׂרֵי בָלָק:

36 וַיִּשְׁמַע בָּלָק כִּי בָא בִלְעָם וַיֵּצֵא לִקְרָאתוֹ אֶל־עִיר מוֹאָב אֲשֶׁר עַל־גְּבוּל אַרְנֹן אֲשֶׁר בִּקְצֵה הַגְּבוּל:

37 וַיֹּאמֶר בָּלָק אֶל־בִּלְעָם הֲלֹא שָׁלֹחַ שָׁלַחְתִּי אֵלֶיךָ לִקְרֹא־לָךְ לָמָּה לֹא־הָלַכְתָּ אֵלָי הַאֻמְנָם לֹא אוּכַל כַּבְּדֶךָ:

38 וַיֹּאמֶר בִּלְעָם אֶל־בָּלָק הִנֵּה־בָאתִי אֵלֶיךָ עַתָּה הֲיָכוֹל אוּכַל דַּבֵּר מְאוּמָה הַדָּבָר אֲשֶׁר יָשִׂים אֱלֹהִים בְּפִי אֹתוֹ אֲדַבֵּר:

39 וַיֵּלֶךְ בִּלְעָם עִם־בָּלָק וַיָּבֹאוּ קִרְיַת חֻצוֹת:

to you?" And he said, "No."

31 Then the LORD opened the eyes of Balaam, and he saw the angel of the LORD standing in the way with his drawn sword in his hand; and he bowed all the way to the ground.

32 The angel of the LORD said to him, "Why have you struck your donkey these three times? Behold, I have come out as an adversary, because your way was contrary to me.

33 "But the donkey saw me and turned aside from me these three times. If she had not turned aside from me, I would surely have killed you just now, and let her live."

40 וַיִּזְבַּח בָּלָק בָּקָר וָצֹאן וַיְשַׁלַּח לְבִלְעָם וְלַשָּׂרִים אֲשֶׁר אִתּוֹ: 41 וַיְהִי בַבֹּקֶר וַיִּקַּח בָּלָק אֶת־בִּלְעָם וַיַּעֲלֵהוּ בָּמוֹת בָּעַל וַיַּרְא מִשָּׁם קְצֵה הָעָם:

³⁴ Balaam said to the angel of the LORD, "I have sinned, for I did not know that you were standing in the way against me. Now then, if it is displeasing to you, I will turn back."

³⁵ But the angel of the LORD said to Balaam, "Go with the men, but you shall speak only the word which I tell you." So Balaam went along with the leaders of Balak.

³⁶ When Balak heard that Balaam was coming, he went out to meet him at the city of Moab, which is on the Arnon border, at the extreme end of the border.

³⁷ Then Balak said to Balaam, "Did I not urgently send to you to

call you? Why did you not come to me? Am I really unable to honor you?"

[38] So Balaam said to Balak, "Behold, I have come now to you! Am I able to speak anything at all? The word that God puts in my mouth, that I shall speak."

[39] And Balaam went with Balak, and they came to Kiriath-huzoth.

[40] Balak sacrificed oxen and sheep, and sent *some* to Balaam and the leaders who were with him.

[41] Then it came about in the morning that Balak took Balaam and brought him up to the high places of Baal, and he saw from there

a portion of the people.	

Process of Discovery

Linguistics Section

Linguistic Structure

A [1] Then the sons of Israel journeyed, and camped in the plains of Moab beyond the Jordan *opposite* Jericho. [2] Now Balak the son of Zippor saw all that Israel had done to the Amorites. [3] So Moab was in great fear because of the people, for they were numerous; and Moab was in dread of the sons of Israel. [4] Moab said to the elders of Midian, "Now this horde will lick up all that is around us, as the ox licks up the grass of the field." And Balak the son of Zippor was king of Moab at that time. [5] So he sent messengers to Balaam the son of Beor, at Pethor, which is near the River, *in* the land of the sons of his people, to call him, saying, "Behold, a people came out of Egypt; behold, they cover the surface of the land, and they are living opposite me. [6] "Now, therefore, please come, curse this people for me since they are too mighty for me; perhaps I may be able to defeat them and drive them out of the land. For I know that he whom you bless is blessed, and he whom you curse is cursed." [7] So the elders of Moab and the elders of Midian departed with the *fees for* divination in their hand; and they came to Balaam and repeated Balak's words to him.

B [8] He said to them, "Spend the night here, and I will bring word back to you as the LORD may speak to me." And the leaders of Moab stayed with Balaam. [9] Then God came to Balaam and said, "Who are these men with you?" [10] Balaam said to God, "Balak the son of Zippor, king of Moab, has sent *word* to me, [11] 'Behold, there is a people who came out of Egypt and they cover the surface of the land; now come, curse them for me; perhaps I may be able to fight against them and drive them out.'" [12] God said to Balaam, "Do not go with them; you shall not curse the people, for they are blessed." [13] So Balaam arose in the morning and said to Balak's leaders, "Go back to your land, for the LORD has refused to let me go with you." [14] The leaders of Moab arose and went to Balak and said, "Balaam refused to come with us."

B' [15] Then Balak again sent leaders, more numerous and more distinguished than the former. [16] They came to Balaam and said to him, "Thus says Balak the son of Zippor, 'Let nothing, I beg you, hinder you from coming to me; [17] for I will indeed honor you richly, and I will do whatever you say to me. Please come then, curse this people for me.'" [18] Balaam replied to the servants of Balak, "Though Balak were to give me his house full of silver and gold, I could not do anything, either small or great, contrary to the command of the LORD my God. [19] "Now please, you also stay here tonight, and I will find out what else the LORD will speak to me." [20] God came to Balaam at night and said to him, "If the men have come to call you, rise up *and* go with them; but only the word which I speak to you shall you do." [21] So Balaam arose in the morning, and saddled his donkey and went with the leaders of Moab. [22] But God was angry because he was going, and the angel of the LORD took his stand in the way as an adversary against him. Now he was riding on his donkey and his two servants were with him. ²³ When the donkey saw the angel of the LORD standing in the way with his drawn sword in his hand, the donkey turned off from the way and went into the field; but Balaam struck the donkey to turn her back into the way. ²⁴ Then the angel of the LORD stood in a narrow path of the vineyards, *with* a wall on this side and a wall on that side. ²⁵ When the donkey saw the angel of the LORD, she pressed herself to the wall and pressed Balaam's foot against the wall, so he struck her again. ²⁶ The angel of the LORD went further, and stood in a narrow place where there was no way to turn to the right hand or the left. ²⁷ When the donkey saw the angel of the LORD, she lay down under Balaam; so Balaam was angry and struck the donkey with his stick. ²⁸ And the LORD opened the mouth of the donkey, and she said to Balaam, "What have I done to you, that you have struck me these three times?" ²⁹ Then Balaam said to the donkey, "Because you have made a mockery of me! If there had been a sword in my hand, I would have killed you by now."

[30] The donkey said to Balaam, "Am I not your donkey on which you have ridden all your life to this day? Have I ever been accustomed to do so to you?" And he said, "No." [31] Then the LORD opened the eyes of Balaam, and he saw the angel of the LORD standing in the way with his drawn sword in his hand; and he bowed all the way to the ground. [32] The angel of the LORD said to him, "Why have you struck your donkey these three times? Behold, I have come out as an adversary, because your way was contrary to me. [33] "But the donkey saw me and turned aside from me these three times. If she had not turned aside from me, I would surely have killed you just now, and let her live." [34] Balaam said to the angel of the LORD, "I have sinned, for I did not know that you were standing in the way against me. Now then, if it is displeasing to you, I will turn back." [35] But the angel of the LORD said to Balaam, "Go with the men, but you shall speak only the word which I tell you." So Balaam went along with the leaders of Balak.

A' [36] When Balak heard that Balaam was coming, he went out to meet him at the city of Moab, which is on the Arnon border, at the extreme end of the border. [37] Then Balak said to Balaam, "Did I not urgently send to you to call you? Why did you not come to me? Am I really unable to honor you?" [38] So Balaam said to Balak, "Behold, I have come now to you! Am I able to speak anything at all? The word that God puts in my mouth, that I shall speak." [39] And Balaam went with Balak, and they came to Kiriath-huzoth. [40] Balak sacrificed oxen and sheep, and sent *some* to Balaam and the leaders who were with him. [41] Then it came about in the morning that Balak took Balaam and brought him up to the high places of Baal, and he saw from there a portion of the people.

Discussion

This chapter contains one chiasm. It is based on the two messages from Balak. In the previous chapter, the Torah describes the battles that Israel had with Sichon and Og. The Israelites were expected to lose the battles, but through the power of the LORD, they won both battles. The plains of Moab, where they were, was considered an effective barrier from an invasion of Moab by any of the peoples of Canaan.[4] With this territory in the hands of Israel, Balak became very concerned that his land would be invaded.

Questioning the Passage

---

[4] Abraham ben Jacob Saba and Eliyahu Munk, *Tzror Hamor: Torah Commentary*, vol. 4 (Jerusalem: Lambda Publishers, 2008).

1. Why did the Israelites camp on the plains of Moab? (v. 1)

The Israelites needed to find an entrance into Canaan. The city of Jericho sat on the trade route between the Via Maris (the coastal road from Israel to Egypt) and the King's Highway (the road that ran from Northern Mesopotamia to southwestern Arabia). The connection between the two roads was a road that ran East to West. On the eastern end of the road sat Jericho. On the western side of the road sat Meggido.

2. Who were the Amorites? (v. 2)

    "Amorite, member of an ancient Semitic-speaking people who dominated the history of Mesopotamia, Syria, and Palestine from about 2000 to about 1600 BC. In the oldest cuneiform sources (*c.* 2400–*c.* 2000 BC), the Amorites were equated with the West, though their true place of origin was most likely Arabia, not Syria. They were troublesome nomads and were believed to be one of the causes of the downfall of the 3rd dynasty of Ur (*c.* 2112–*c.* 2004 BC)."[5]

---

[5] The Editors of Encyclopaedia Britannica, "Amorite," Encyclopædia Britannica (Encyclopædia Britannica, inc., April 17, 2014), https://www.britannica.com/topic/Amorite.

3. Who were the Moabites? (v. 2)

    "In the Bible, the Moabites are said to have descended from Moab, the son of Lot and his oldest daughter (Genesis 19:37). The kingdom of Moab stretched "north and south of the Arnon River" with its capital at Dibon. The Moabites worshiped the god Chemosh, who may be depicted in the Balua' Stele (dated to the end of Late Bronze Age). The most famous Moabite king—from the archaeological record at least—is Mesha. The large inscription he left behind is the longest Moabite text. Dating to the ninth century B.C.E., the Mesha Stele describes how

King Mesha rescued the Moabites from Israelite rule."[6]

4. Why did Moab talk about Israel to the elders of Midian? (v. 4)

"Moab was a land, a people, and a kingdom located east of the Dead Sea in what is now the kingdom of Jordan. Moab as a land is first mentioned in the reign of the Egyptian pharaoh Ramses II (circa 1270 B.C.E.). The kingdom of Moab emerged in the ninth century B.C.E. and disappeared a few decades after the destruction of

---

[6] "Who Were the Ammonites, Moabites and Edomites in the Bible?," Biblical Archaeology Society, May 3, 2019, https://www.biblicalarchaeology.org/daily/ancient-cultures/ancient-near-eastern-world/ammonites-moabites-edomites-in-the-bible/.

Jerusalem by the Babylonian king Nebuchadnezzar II in 586 B.C.E."[7]

The nation of Moab was relatively new. They did not have time to create a large population. The Israelites had spent four hundred years in Egypt and were fruitful and multiplied. In ancient times wars were won by the side with the larger and the braver army. The army of Israel was huge when compared to Moab. Therefore, Moab needed to find an ally if they intended to defeat Israel.

---

[7] "Moab by Bruce Routledge," Moab, accessed February 24, 2020, https://www.bibleodyssey.org/en/places/main-articles/moab.

It is interesting that Balak, King of Moab, decided to talk with Midian. Since Moses' father-in-law was Jethro, a leader of Midian, it was unlikely that Midian would ally itself with Moab against Israel. It is possible that Balak was unaware of the family connection between Israel and Midian. The Tzror Hamor (a commentary on the Torah) says that a central king did not rule Midian then.[8] The phrase "the elders of Midian" supports the cultural aspect of Midian.

The Chumash says that Moab spoke with Midian elders to learn all they

---

[8] Abraham ben Jacob Saba and Eliyahu Munk, Tzror Hamor: Torah Commentary, vol. 4 (Jerusalem: Lambda Publishers, 2008).

could about Israel. Moab needed to discover how Israel, a nation under slavery, became such a mighty nation. Since Moses spent a great deal of time living in Midian, the elders of Midian might have known of his strengths and thinking.[9]

The Targum Pseudo-Jonathan says, "And Balak bar Zippor, a Midianite, was the king of Moab at that time; without (a Midianite) being such at another time; for so was the tradition among them, to have kings from this people and from that, by turns. (Num. 22:4 PJE)."[10] The Targum indicates

---

[9] Nosson Scherman, The Chumash: the Torah: Haftaros and Five Megillos with a Commentary Anthologized from the Rabbinic Writings (Brooklyn, NY: Mesorah Pub., 1994).
[10] Targum Pseudo-Jonathan from Bibleworks V.10.

that Balak contacted Midian since he was a Midianite.

5. What does it mean to "lick up" everything? (v. 4)

    This phrase is an idiom, meaning that Israel uprooted and utterly destroyed everything in its path. The Moabites feared that if Israel attacked their nation that there would not be anything left to Moab when they left.[11]

6. What river is the River in verse five?

    The Targum Onkelos and Yonasan say that the "River" is the Euphrates.[12]

---

[11] IBID.

[12] Nosson Scherman, The Chumash: the Torah: Haftaros and Five Megillos with a Commentary Anthologized from the Rabbinic Writings (Brooklyn, NY: Mesorah Pub., 1994).

7. Why did Balak summon Balaam? (v. 5)

Balak came from the land of Aram. Balaam lived in Aram and had prophesied that Balak would become a king. Balak knew about Balaam's power and summoned him to curse the Israelites.[13]

8. What did it mean to offer a curse? (v. 6)

A curse was the invoking of God's wrath upon a nation. Balak believed that Balaam's curse would weaken Israel in such a manner that he could easily conquer the people.

---

[13] IBID.

9. What is the fee for divination? (v. 7)

    Another translation of this verse can read "charms in their hands." The Zohar (Jewish book of mysticism) in Chadash says that Balaam and Balak were experts in the art of the occult. Balaam practiced the art with his eyes and mouth. Balak practiced the black arts with his hands utilizing charms. Balak would have dispatched messengers to go to Balaam using charms of divination.

10. Why did Balaam want to speak with the LORD? (v. 8)

    It was believed that all prophecy came from the LORD. Balaam could not offer a prophecy of a curse against

Israel without the LORD's permission. That is the usual answer to this question. A problem with this answer is, did Balaam know anything about the God of Israel? He was from Aram. Perhaps he had a family connection to Terah, Abraham's father, and learned about the LORD who spoke to Abraham. That may be considered a bit of a stretch. It is unlikely that the nations of the Middle East knew anything about the LORD before Moses and Israel had returned to the land. The verse would make more sense if it said that Balaam had to speak with his god about the curse he was asking to put upon Israel.

Balaam told the messengers from Balak that the LORD told him he was not to go with them. The messengers returned to Balak to tell the king what Balaam said. Balak then sent a more extensive and stronger messenger to Balaam to come to him. Again Balaam asked the LORD whether he should go. The LORD told him to go with the men.

11. Why did the LORD tell Balaam to go with the men to curse Israel? (v. 20) The LORD's permission and then anger is difficult to interpret. The sage Rashi[i] said since the LORD used the word לְךָ that, the LORD said that Balaam could go if he thought it would be a benefit for him. Balak

undoubtedly offered payment for Balaam's work. However, the LORD told Balaam that he could only speak what the LORD told him. The LORD allowed Balaam the free will to go. Balaam was a greedy man, and the LORD knew it. Balaam found it challenging to resist the temptation of money.

The sage Ramban[ii] said that the LORD told Balaam that he was not to curse Israel. Balaam told Balak's emissaries this. Balak knew of Balaam's greed, so he sent higher-ranking officials to see

Balaam and a larger "reward" for cursing Israel.[14]

12. Why was the LORD angry at Balaam for going with the men when He told him to do this? (v. 22)

The LORD was angry with Balaam even though he was permitted to go. As noted in the previous question, the LORD was testing Balaam to see if his desire for money and to satisfy his hatred of Israel was stronger than obeying the LORD. Balaam demonstrated that his greed and hatred were stronger than his following the word of the LORD.

---

[14] Nosson Scherman, The Chumash: the Torah: Haftaros and Five Megillos with a Commentary Anthologized from the Rabbinic Writings (Brooklyn, NY: Mesorah Pub., 1994).

Balaam knew that he could not help Balak. He could not pronounce a curse against Israel when the LORD told him he did not have permission to do it. A lesson here is that every person has free will. A person's actions demonstrate his/her true faith and obedience to the LORD.

13. What is the angel of the LORD? (v. 22)

The angel of the LORD was sent from the side of mercy and grace (see the entry מַלְאַךְ יְהוָה in the Phrase Study section).

14. Is there a significance that the donkey was female? (v. 25)

Female donkeys were used for riding, while male donkeys were used for carrying freight.

15. What is the significance of the donkey speaking to Balaam? (v. 28)

The typical western view of the story is that the she-donkey could speak because the LORD made it happen. This western interpretation leads to the understanding that everything is possible for the LORD. Indeed, the universe's creator and all it contains could make a donkey talk. However, the LORD does not often upset His world's natural balance. Also, the Scripture is a Semitic document, not a western document. The authors of the Scripture used their culture and methods of writing. Creating allegorical stories for the lesson to be learned is how teaching occurred. Therefore, the story should not be taken as a literal story. Many Christian commentators using their western view, will say that one cannot take parts of the Scripture and read it literally and others allegorically. They say the Scripture must be read in one way. Martin Luther led the Protestant interpretation charge when he said that the Scripture must be read literally. Too bad the Scripture was not written literally but rather allegorically. Luther's comment was based on his western learning. The Scripture is not a western document and cannot be looked at that way.

The Chumash likes to express this story as a miracle of the LORD to show Balaam that even man's normal functions, such as the ability to speak, are under the LORD's control. If the LORD could force a beast to speak, then the LORD could force him to say what the LORD wanted. The Sage Ramban said that this event proves that human sorcery can not prevail against the LORD.

16. Why did Balaam not see the angel of the LORD? (v. 31)

A simple answer is that Balaam was not used to seeing an angel of the LORD. Another view is that Balaam was not looking for the LORD. He assumed that what he was doing was correct and that nothing would stop him.

17. Is there a significance that Balaam struck the donkey three times? (v. 32) Unfortunately, the donkey was struck three times. The number three signifies that the divine is involved. The LORD was trying to get Balaam's attention through the donkey. He did not sense that what he was doing was not something the LORD wanted him to do. Three times tells the reader that the message that the angel brought was divine.

Biblical Personalities

1. Balak was the son of Zippor who was the king of the Moabites.

2. Balaam was the son of Pethor - "Balaam, son of Beor, was a prophet from Penthor, on the Euphrates River."[15]

---

[15] Balaam and Balak, accessed February 22, 2020, http://www.aboutbibleprophecy.com/p166.htm.

Biblical Locations

1. Plains of Moab[16]

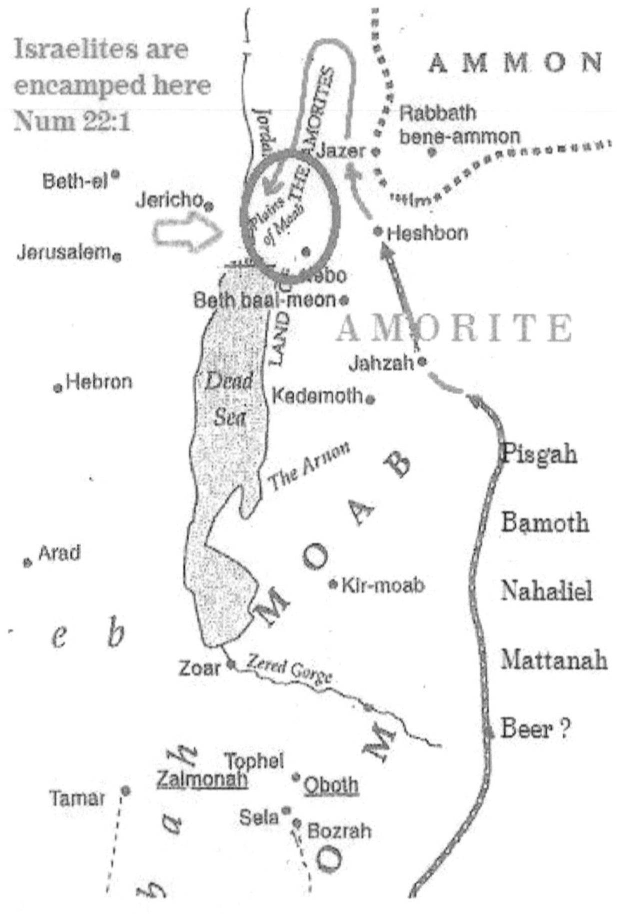

---

[16] Steven DiMattei, "#288. Where Are the Israelites: on the Plains of Moab OR on the Border of Moab? (Num 22:1 vs Num 22:3-5)," Contradictions in the Bible, March 2, 2015,

2. Pethor[17]

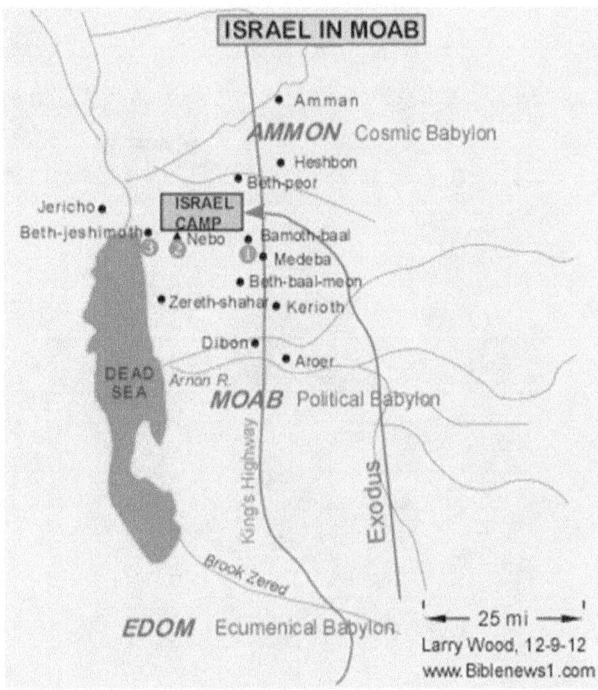

accessed February 22, 2020,
http://contradictionsinthebible.com/plains-of-moab-or-
border-of-moab/.
[17] Index of /maps, accessed February 22, 2020,
http://www.biblenews1.com/maps/.

3. Arnon[18]

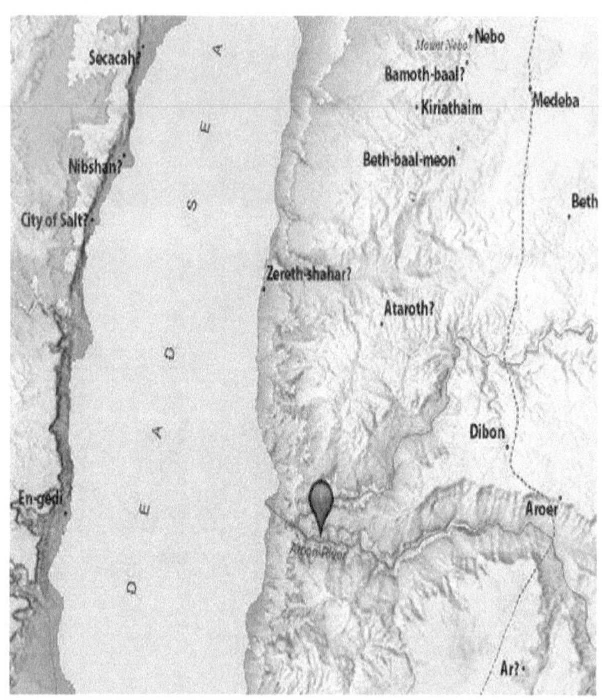

---

[18] "Visualizing Isaiah 15-16: the Fords of the Arnon in Moab," Ferrell's Travel Blog, February 24, 2014, https://ferrelljenkins.blog/2014/02/24/visualizing-isaiah-15-16-the-fords-of-the-arnon-in-moab/.

4. Kiriath-huzoth[19]

---

[19] Bible Map: Kiriath-baal (Kiriath-jearim), accessed February 22, 2020, https://bibleatlas.org/kiriath-baal.htm.

Phrase Study

1. קָסַם. "Divination, witchcraft, sorcery, fortune telling, omen, lot, orack, decision. The exact meaning of this variety of occultism is unknown. That fact accounts for the variety of translations. The account in Ezek 21:21–22 [H 27–28] is the only clue to exactly how קָסַם may have been practiced. Shaking or flinging down arrows, consulting teraphim, and hepatoscopy (looking at the liver) may be subcategories of קָסַם. In any event, verse 22 [H 28] uses קָסַם as if it were one of the arrows to be thrown down. In fact, the NEB translates the word as "augur's arrow" and the NAB as "divining arrow." The JB uses "omen" and "lot" in these two verses.

Another interesting use of קֶסֶם is at Num 22:7, where the word seems to indicate a "reward" or "fee" for "divination" (Berkeley Version, sorcery; Amplified, foretelling; NEB, augury) to be paid to Balaam. Later in that account (23:23) קֶסֶם is parallel to נַחַשׁ (cf. 2 Kgs 17:17). In Jer 14:14 it is parallel to "lying vision," "a thing of nought," and "self-deceit" (cf. Ezek 13:6, 23).

A third noteworthy passage is Prov 16:10. There the AV has "divine sentence," the RSV "inspired decisions," and the JB, NEB, and NAB "oracles.." Whereas קֶסֶם is generally forbidden (Deut 18:10), or only used by non-Israelites, in Prov 16:10 it seems perfectly permissible and commendable. The best known occurrence of קֶסֶם is in 1 Sam 15:23, where Samuel confronts Saul for disobedience in the matter of the spoils from the Amalekite victory. The prophet declared:

To obey is better than sacrifice and to hearken than the fat of rams. For rebellion is as the sin of קֶסֶם.

The traditional rendering "witchcraft" is followed by the ASV, Amplified and the NEB, while the JB has "sorcery" and the Berkeley Version has "fortune-telling.""""[20]

---

[20] R. Laird Harris, Gleason L. Archer, and Bruce K. Waltke, Theological Wordbook of the Old Testament (Chicago: Moody Press, 2004).

2. מַלְאַךְ יְהוָה - "an angel of the LORD." An angel of the LORD means the angel was from the Sefirah[iii] Chesed, meaning the angel was to bring the LORD's mercy to Balaam. "An angel of God" means the angel is from the Sefirah Gevurah, meaning the angel was to bring justice. Even though the LORD was not happy with Balaam's decision to go, the LORD was going to show him mercy.

Culture Section

Questioning the passage

1. Why did Balaam saddle his donkey in verse twenty-one?

In Balaam's day, a man of his stature did not saddle his donkey. Instead, a servant did this for him. The Sages in Sanhedrin (a book of the Talmud) said that Balaam hated Israel to the point that his dignity would not stop him. He got up early in the morning before his servants and saddled his donkey to leave as quickly as possible.

2. Why did Balaam hate the Israelites?

"It is precisely this question which led the biblical commentator Rashi to conclude that "Balaam detested the Jews more than Balak." Balak hated the Jews for a good reason; in his estimation, they presented a mortal threat to him and his citizens. Balaam, on the other hand, like so many anti-Semites throughout the ages, hated the Jews for no reason at all. It was essential hate that defied rhyme or reason—a hate that was qualitatively greater than Balak's. And as such, he jumped at the opportunity to curse the Jews, though he knew well that Balak's fear was groundless."[21]

[21] Naftali Silberberg, "A Love (From) Hate Relationship," Judaism, May 24, 2010, access February 24, 2020, https://www.chabad.org/parshah/article_cdo/aid/1216903/jewish/A-Love-From-Hate-Relationship.htm.

The Talking Donkey as an Allegorical Story

The talking donkey should be viewed as an allegorical story since the Scripture was written by Semitic people who learned about the ways of the LORD and their history through allegorical stories. The story of Balaam and the talking donkey is a straightforward story to pass down through the generations. The story's lessons become memorable because they are associated with a story. In today's language, one could say, "a talking donkey, well, that is cool." Indeed the Shriek movies had a talking donkey in it. When watching that movie, do viewers believe a donkey can talk? The story is memorable because the lessons of the movie come from an ogre and a talking donkey. The same thing is happening with this allegorical story.

The story's lesson is that the LORD desires us to follow His ways and direction. The LORD created the universe for us to live in and to learn about His ways. Balaam spoke to the LORD about going with Balak's messengers to curse Israel. The LORD told Him he should not allow greed to overtake his good sense. However, the LORD allowed Balaam to use his free will. The greed in Balaam was more potent than the Word of the LORD. Balaam started on his travels to Balak when the LORD sent an angel of mercy to stop him. Even though Balaam disobeyed the LORD, the LORD showed

Balaam mercy. We can learn here that each person may use their free will as they wish; however, when a free will goes against a plan of the LORD, the LORD will let us know. It will still be free will that prevails, but hopefully, the person will see that the LORD's way is the best and will abandon their way.

Another lesson is that our gifts and talents are from the LORD. It is the LORD who gave Balaam the ability to offer prophecy. Balaam was able to offer prophecy so that he could bless Israel (comes in chapters 21 and 22). The gift was for the LORD's usage and not Balaam. Therefore, the gifts and talents that the LORD gives a person should be primarily used for the LORD's purpose and not the individual's purpose alone. It seems fine to use the LORD's gifts and talents to better oneself as long as the gifts are used for the LORD's plans. The LORD's plans and an individual's desire can coexist simultaneously and in harmony. If the harmony is broken, then the LORD will prevail. This breakage is seen in the Balaam story because the angel of the LORD stopped Balaam in his journey to see Balak.

A third lesson is that it is advantageous to recognize the power of the LORD. The LORD sends His angels to Earth to help individuals live better lives. How many people miss messages from the LORD that would greatly help them in their lives? Today people are so busy running around from place to place that they do not take the time to sit back to listen to the LORD and to see the LORD giving them directions. Balaam became so intent on cursing Israel that he did not see the Angel of the Lord blocking his way. Finally, his donkey speaks up out of fear. The Angel of the Lord was holding a sword that could have killed the donkey. Sometimes people need a good slap to the side of their head to realize that the LORD is speaking to them.

There are angels of the LORD all around us. If a person wants to hear the LORD speaking, it is essential to find time to listen, meaning removing all distractions. The angels of the LORD can be seen if looked for. A person must want to find the LORD's angels and receive their message. It also takes time. Just saying, "LORD speak to me" does not mean an immediate answer is given. Also, the answer may have been given, but the recipient of the message does not know how to hear and receive the message. It takes practice to learn how to recognize the LORD's angels and hear the LORD's voice.

Ancient people knew how to listen to the voice of the LORD. The Aramaic word for prayer is *slota*. This word is derived from the root word *slot*. The root word means to trap. Therefore, to pray, *slota,* means to listen for the LORD's voice. An excellent reading resource about ancient prayer is <u>Setting a Trap for God</u> by Rocco Errico. Prayer is an attempt to hear the LORD speaking. How can people today claim that they are following the ways of the LORD when they do not take the time to listen to the LORD's voice? When the LORD's Word is heard, it is expected to be followed.

A talking donkey is unnecessary to know whether a person is following the LORD's Word. Numerous resources are available to learn how to listen for the LORD's voice and respond to it. It is recommended that if the reader wants to learn more, it would be best to seek out a Spiritual Director.

Michael Harvey Koplitz

Bibliography

2019. *Amorite - Encyclopedia Britannica.* May 3. Accessed February 24, 2020. https://www.britannica.com/topic/Amorite.

2020. *Balaam and Balak.* February: 22.

n.d. *Bible Map: Kiriath-baal.* Accessed February 22, 2020. https://bibleatlas.org/kiriath-baal.htm.

1986. *Back to School.* Directed by James Signorelli. Performed by Rodney Dangerfield.

Davis, Anne Kimball. 2012. *The Synoptic Gospels.* Albuquerque.

DiMattei, Steven. 2015. *#288. Where are the Israelites: in the Plains of Moab or on the Border of Moab.* March 2. Accessed February 22, 2020. http://contradictionsinthebible.com/plains-of-moab-or-border-of-moab/.

Munk, Abraham ben Jacob Saba and Eliyahu. 2008. *Tzror Hamor: Torah Commentary Volume 4.* Jerusalem, Israel: Lambda Publishers.

R. Laird Harris, Gleason L. Archer, and Bruce K Waltke. 2004. *Theological Wordbook of the Old Testament.* Chicago, IL: Moody Press.

Routledge, Bruce. n.d. *Moab.* Accessed February 24, 2020. https://www.bibleodyssey.org/en/places/main-articles/moab.

Scherman, Nosson. 1994. *The Chumash: the Torah: the Haftoros and Five Megillos.* Brooklyn, NY: Mesorah Publishing.

Silberberg, Naftali. 2010. *A Love (from) Hate Relationship.* May 24. Accessed February 24, 2020. https://www.chabad.org/parshah/article_cdo/aid/1216903/jewish/A-Love-From-Hate-Relationship.htm.

n.d. *Visualizing Isaiah 15-16: the Fords of the Arnon in Moab.* Accessed February 22, 2020. https://ferrelljenkins.blog/2014/02/24/visualizing-isaiah-15-16-the-fords-of-the-arnon-in-moab/.

2019. *Who were the Ammonites, Moabites and Edomities in the Bible.* May 3. Accessed February 24, 2020. https://www.biblicalarchaeology.org/d

aily/ancient-cultures/ancient-near-eastern-world/ammonites-moabites-edomites-in-the-bible/.

Endnotes

---

[i] "Shlomo Yitzchaki (Hebrew: רבי שלמה יצחקי; Latin: Salomon Isaacides; French: Salomon de Troyes, 22 February 1040 – 13 July 1105), today generally known by the acronym Rashi (Hebrew: רש"י, RAbbi SHlomo Itzhaki), was a medieval French rabbi and author of a comprehensive commentary on the Talmud and commentary on the Tanakh. Acclaimed for his ability to present the basic meaning of the text in a concise and lucid fashion, Rashi appeals to both learned scholars and beginner students, and his works remain a centerpiece of contemporary Jewish study. His commentary on the Talmud, which covers nearly all of the Babylonian Talmud (a total of 30 out of 39

tractates, due to his death), has been included in every edition of the Talmud since its first printing by Daniel Bomberg in the 1520s. His commentary on Tanakh—especially on the Chumash ("Five Books of Moses")—serves as the basis for more than 300 "supercommentaries" which analyze Rashi's choice of language and citations, penned by some of the greatest names in rabbinic literature." Source: https://en.wikipedia.org/wiki/Rashi

[ii] "The sad plight of the Jewish people in Northern France in the days of Rabbi Jechiel of Paris, spread rapidly to the south, until it affected even Spain, the land of culture and learning of that time. But once again the Jewish people found a great champion, who pleaded

their cause and defended their faith against a cruel attack. This great champion was Rabbi Moses ben Nachman Gerondi, known by the abbreviation RaMBaN, and to the non-Jewish world-as Nachmanides. He was called Gerondi after his native town Gerona, Spain, where he was born in the year 4954 (1195 c.e.). He was born of a noble family, which included many prominent Talmudists." Source: https://www.chabad.org/library/article_cdo/aid/111857/jewish/Ramban.htm

iii "There are 10 sefirot, linked in a complex figure that some have called the "Tree of Life," significantly a phrase also often used to refer to the Torah . They are Keter (Crown), Hokhmah (Wisdom), Binah (Understanding), Hesed

(Lovingkindness), Gevurah (Might) or Din (Judgment), Tiferet (Beauty), Hod (Splendor), Netzah (Victory), Yesod (Foundation), and Malkhut (Sovereignty) or Shekhinah (the Divine Presence). Each of them represents one aspect of the Godhead, a facet of the powers of the All Powerful. Each is also identified with a part of the body or aspects of the human personality, a color, and one of the Names of the Holy One.

The relationship of the sefirot looks something like this:

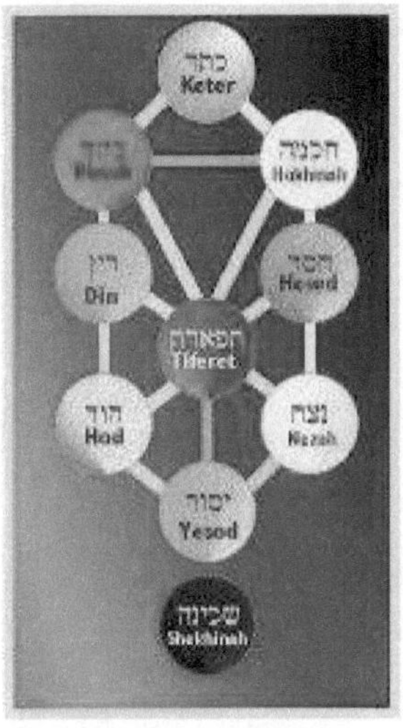

As you can see from the diagram, the attributes of God are highly interdependent, with each one linked to several others. (According to the kabbalists of Safed, each of the ten sefirot contains within it all of the others [i.e., each sefirah represents a piece of a totality and contains an image of this totality within itself].) By understanding their interrelationship, we can understand in some small way the process of The Creation itself." Source: https://www.myjewishlearning.com/article/sefirot/

www.ingramcontent.com/pod-product-compliance
Lightning Source LLC
Chambersburg PA
CBHW051758130726
47987CB00003B/1020